Symphony No. 8
in B Minor, D759
("Unfinished")

&

Symphony No. 9
in C Major, D944
("The Great")

Franz Schubert

From the Breitkopf & Härtel Complete Works Edition

Edited by Johannes Brahms

DOVER PUBLICATIONS, INC.
Mineola, New York

Published in Canada by General Publishing Company, Ltd., 30 Lesmill Road, Don Mills, Toronto, Ontario.
Published in the United Kingdom by Constable and Company, Ltd., 3 The Lanchesters, 162–164 Fulham Palace Road, London W6 9ER.

Bibliographical Note

This Dover edition, first published in 1997, is an unabridged republication of two sections from "Serie 1. Symphonien für Orchester" of *Franz Schubert's Werke. Kritisch durchgesehene Gesammtausgabe,* originally published by Breitkopf & Härtel, Leipzig, 1884–85.

International Standard Book Number: 0-486-29923-6

Manufactured in the United States of America
Dover Publications, Inc., 31 East 2nd Street, Mineola, N.Y. 11501

CONTENTS

"D" numbers refer to entries in *The Schubert Thematic Catalogue,* by Otto Erich Deutsch in collaboration with Donald R. Wakeling, Dover, 1995 (0-486-28685-1). The "Unfinished" was originally published as Symphony No. 7; "The Great," as Symphony No. 8.

Symphony No. 8
in B Minor, D759
("Unfinished")
(1822)

&

Symphony No. 9
in C Major, D944
("The Great")
(1828)

INSTRUMENTATION

2 Flutes [Flauti]
2 Oboes [Oboi]
2 Clarinets [Clarinetti]
For No. 8: "in A"
For No. 9: "in C, A"

2 Bassoons [Fagotti]

2 Horns [Corni]
For No. 8: "in D, E"
For No. 9: "in C"

2 Trumpets [Trombe]
For No. 8: "in E"
For No. 9: "in C, A"

3 Trombones [Tromboni
(Alto, Tenore, Basso)]

Timpani

Violins I, II [Violino]
Violas [Viola]
Cellos [Violoncello]
Basses [Basso]

Symphony No. 8

in B Minor, D759

("Unfinished")

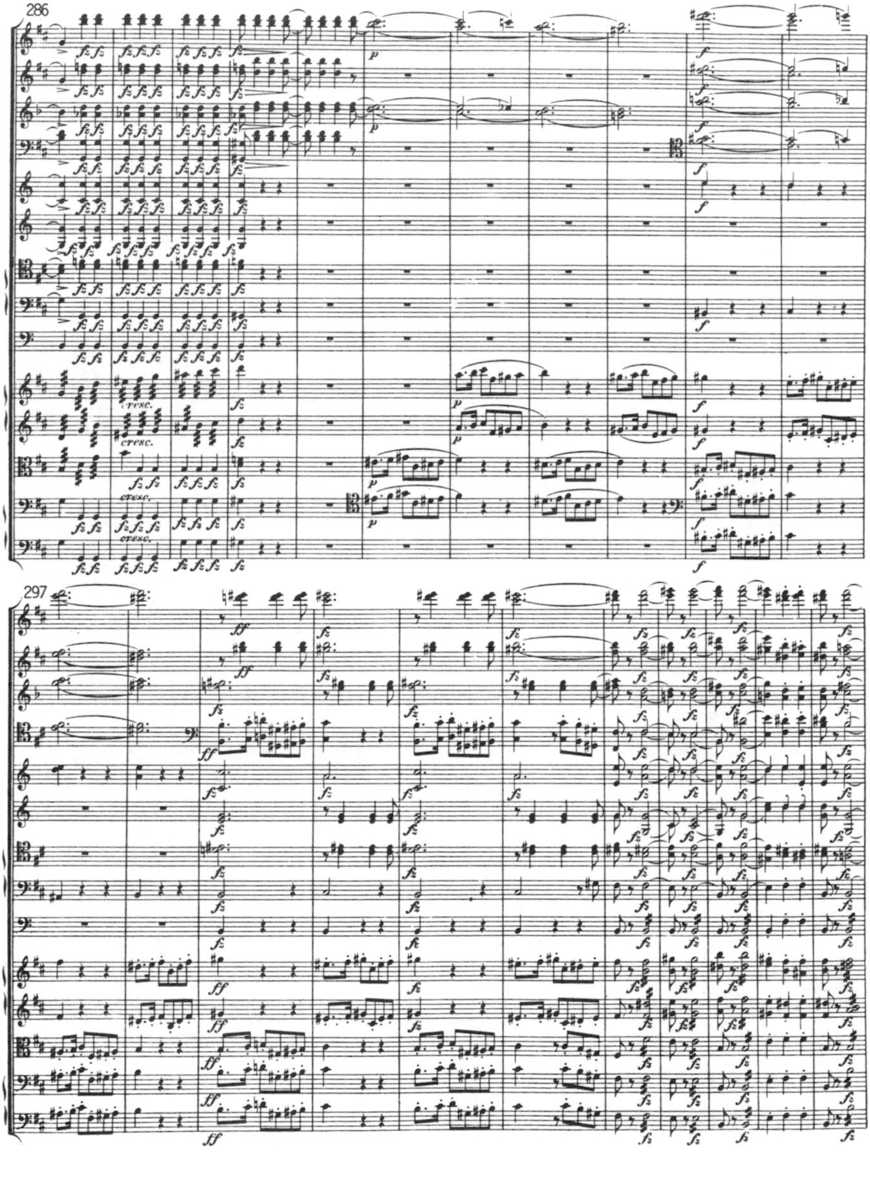
286
cresc.
cresc.
cresc.
cresc.
297

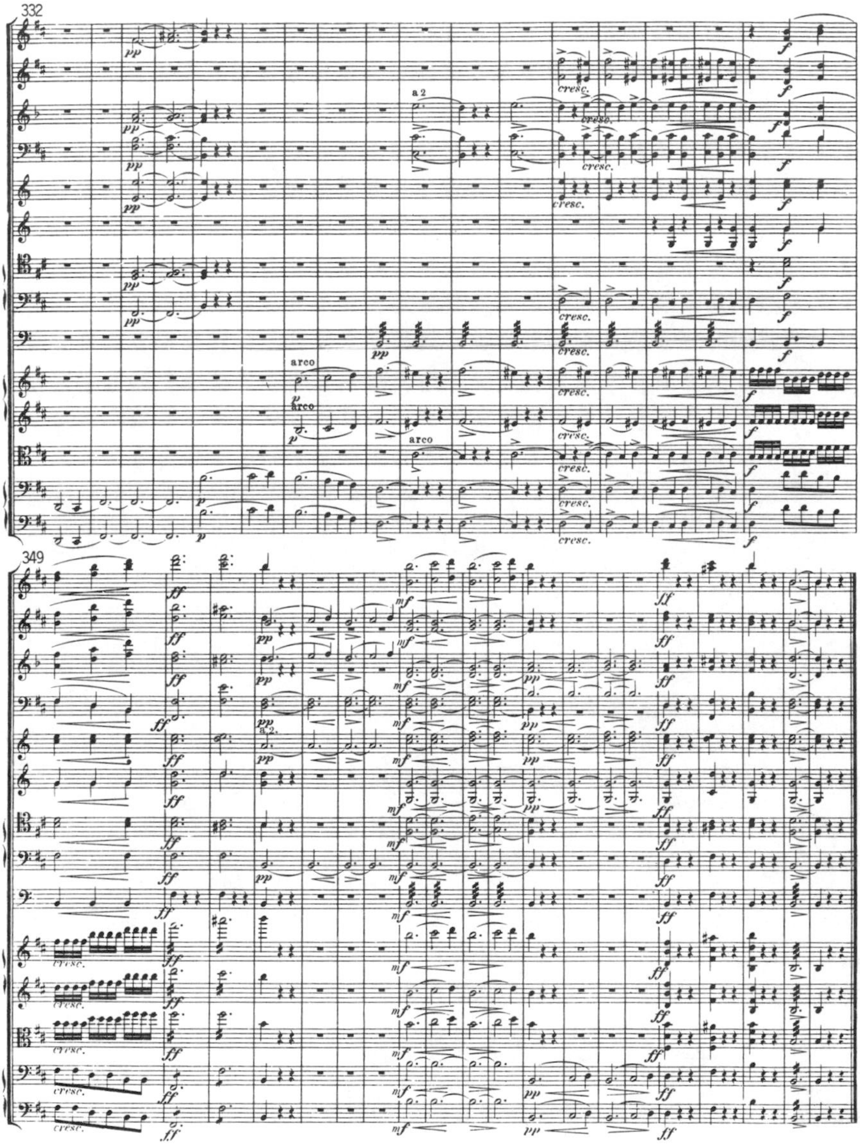
332
pp
a 2
cresc.
arco
p
f
349
ff
mf
a 2.

58
pp
ppp
ppp
pp
pp
pp
pizz.
ppp
72
f
p
pp
dim.
morendo
f
p
pp
dim.
ppp
f
p
pp
dim.
ppp
f
arco
p
pp
dim.
ppp
f
p
pp
pp
ppp

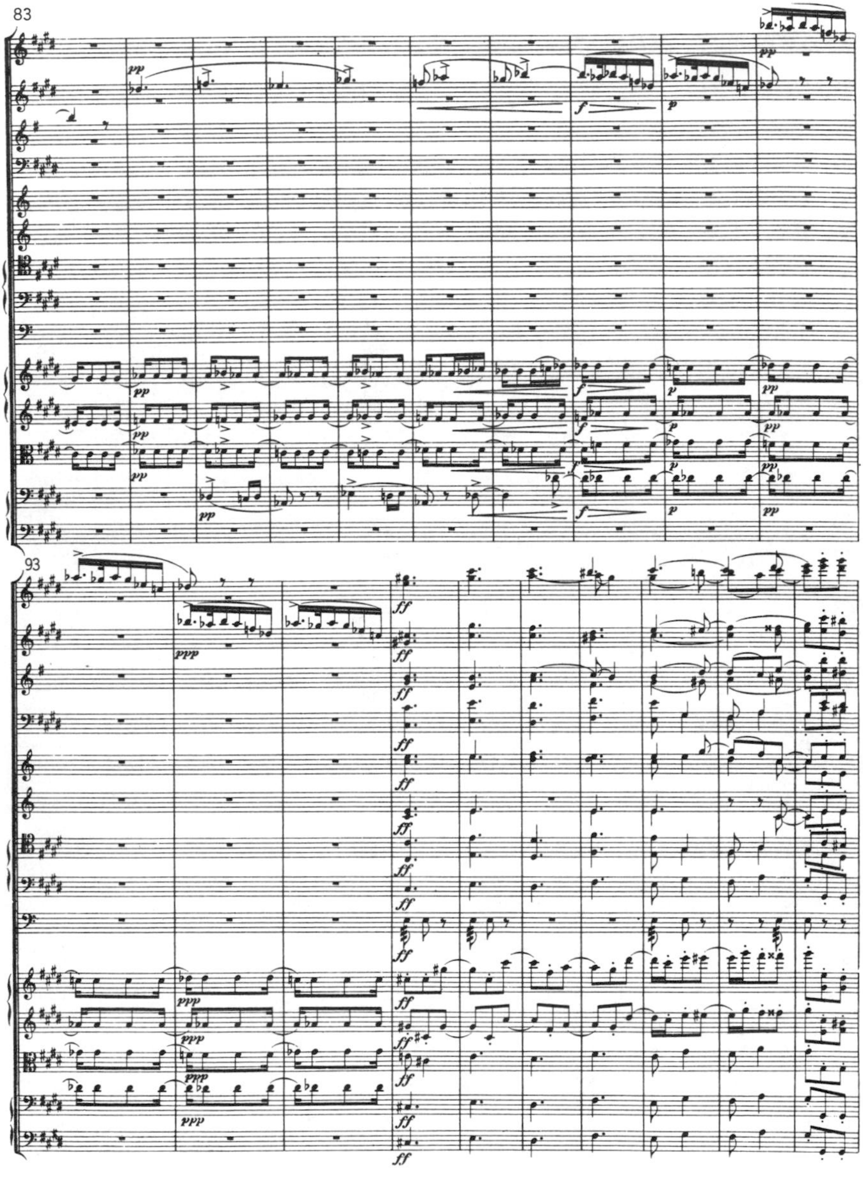
83
93

117

127

138

155

Symphony No. 9

in C Major, D944

("The Great")

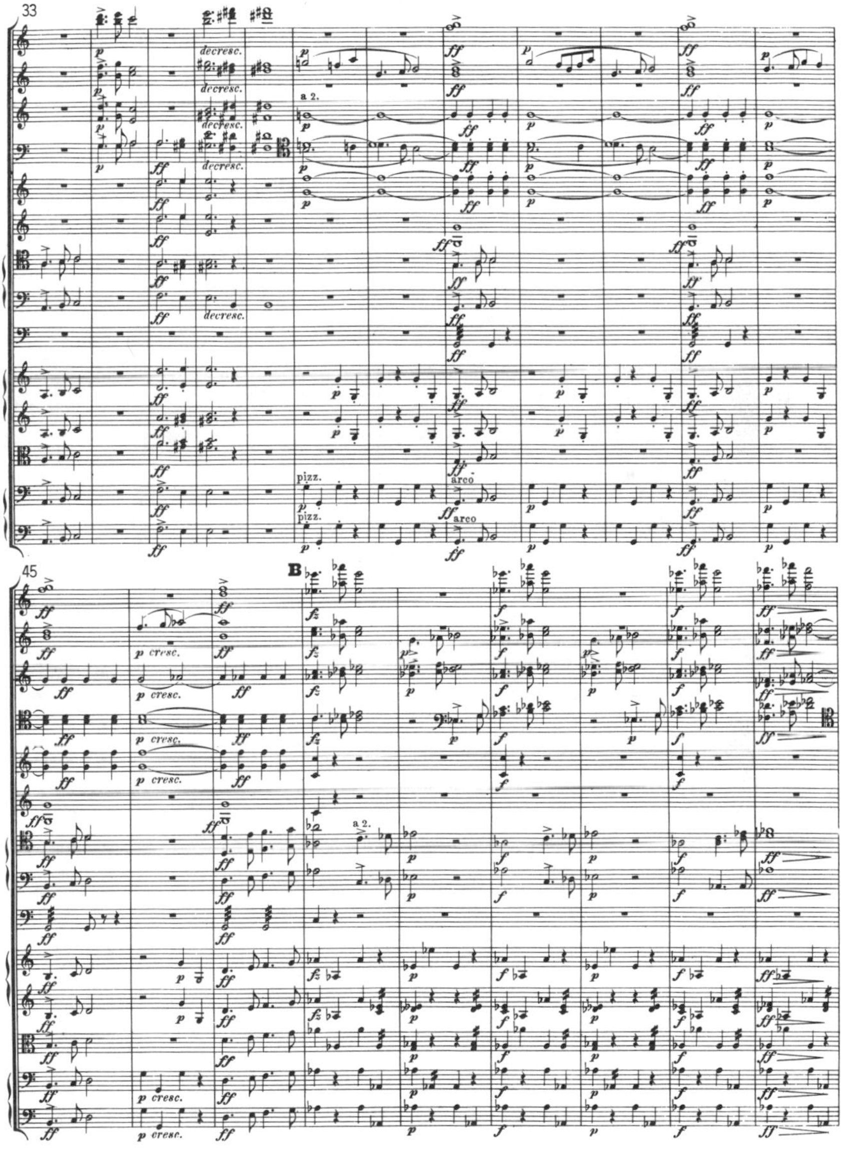
33
decresc.
a 2.
pizz.
arco
45
B
p cresc.

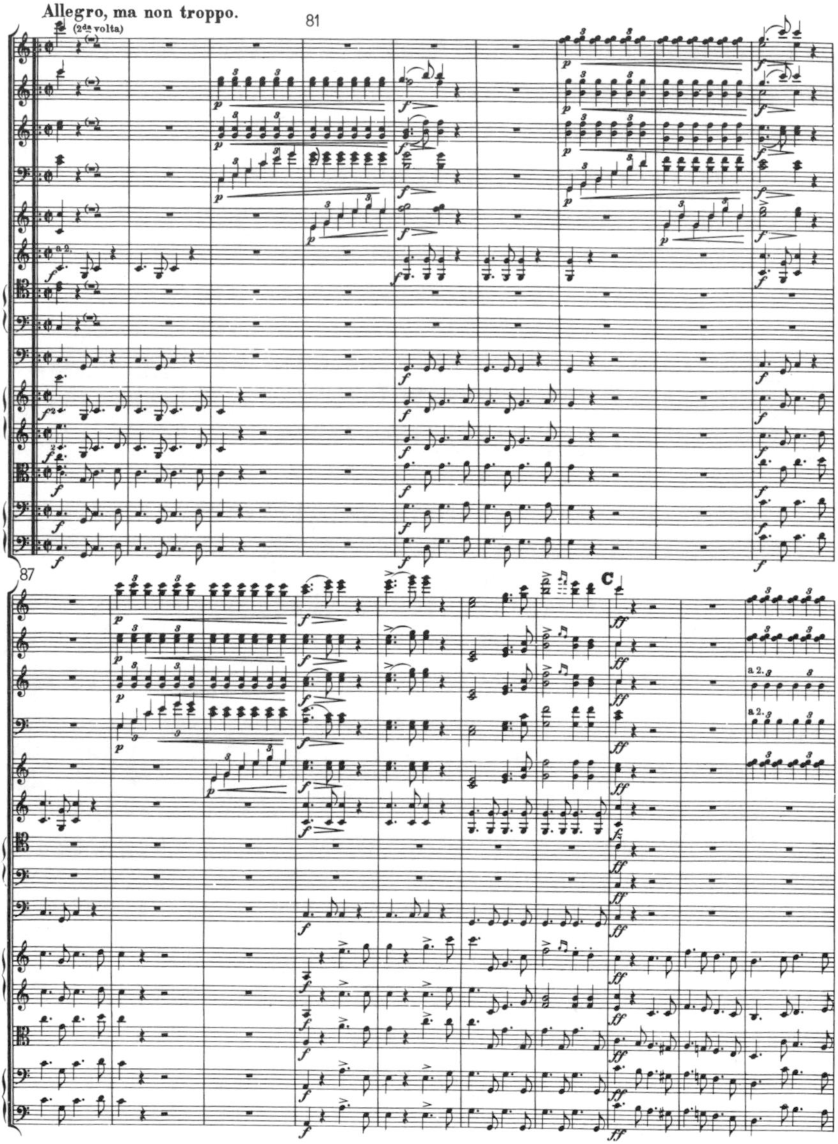
Allegro, ma non troppo.
(2da volta)
81
87
C
a 2.

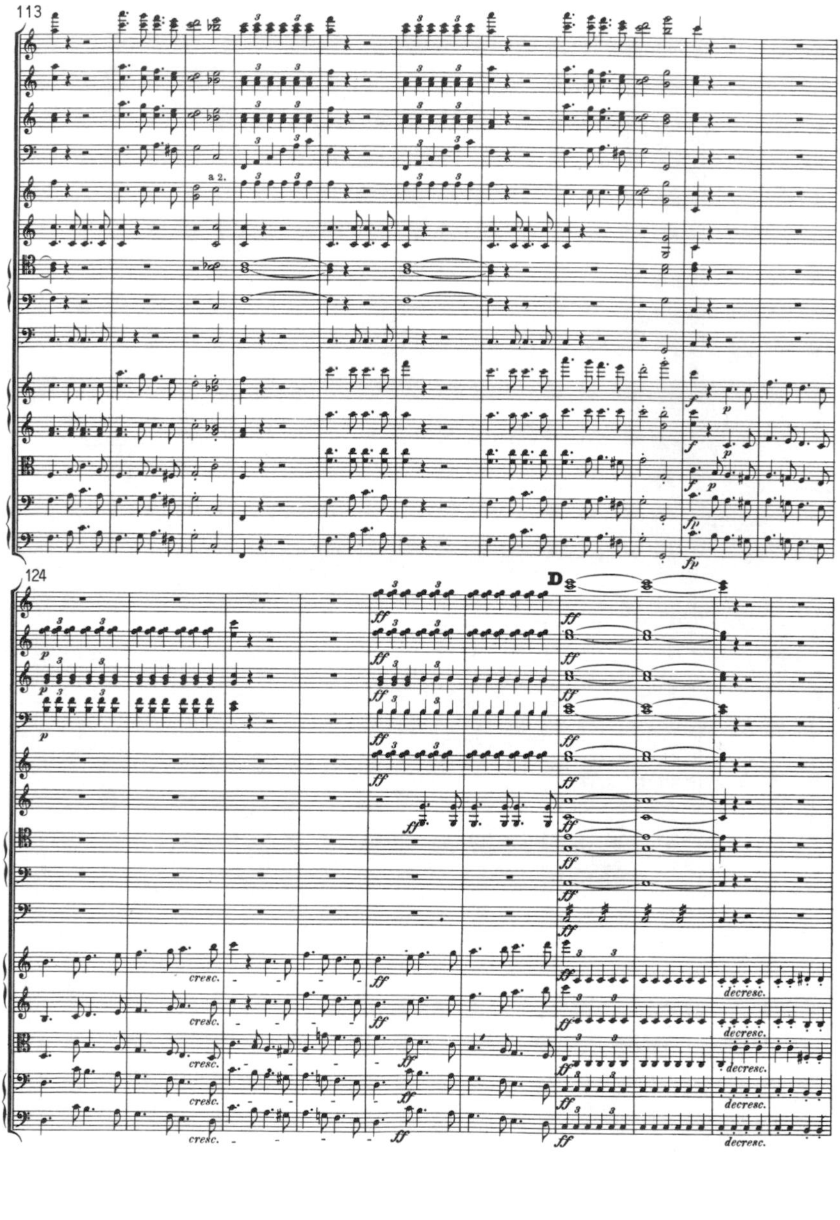
113
a 2.
p
f
fp
124
D
ff
cresc.
decresc.

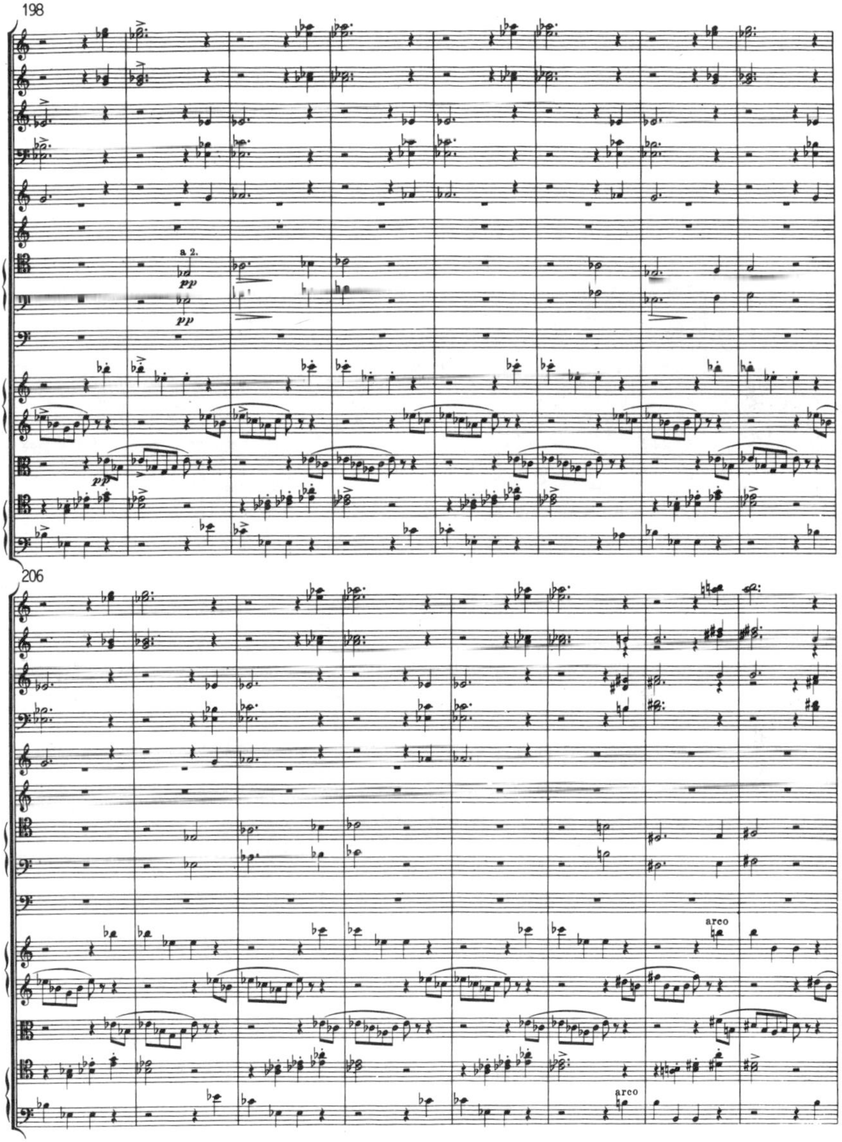
198
a 2.
pp
pp
pp
206
arco
arco

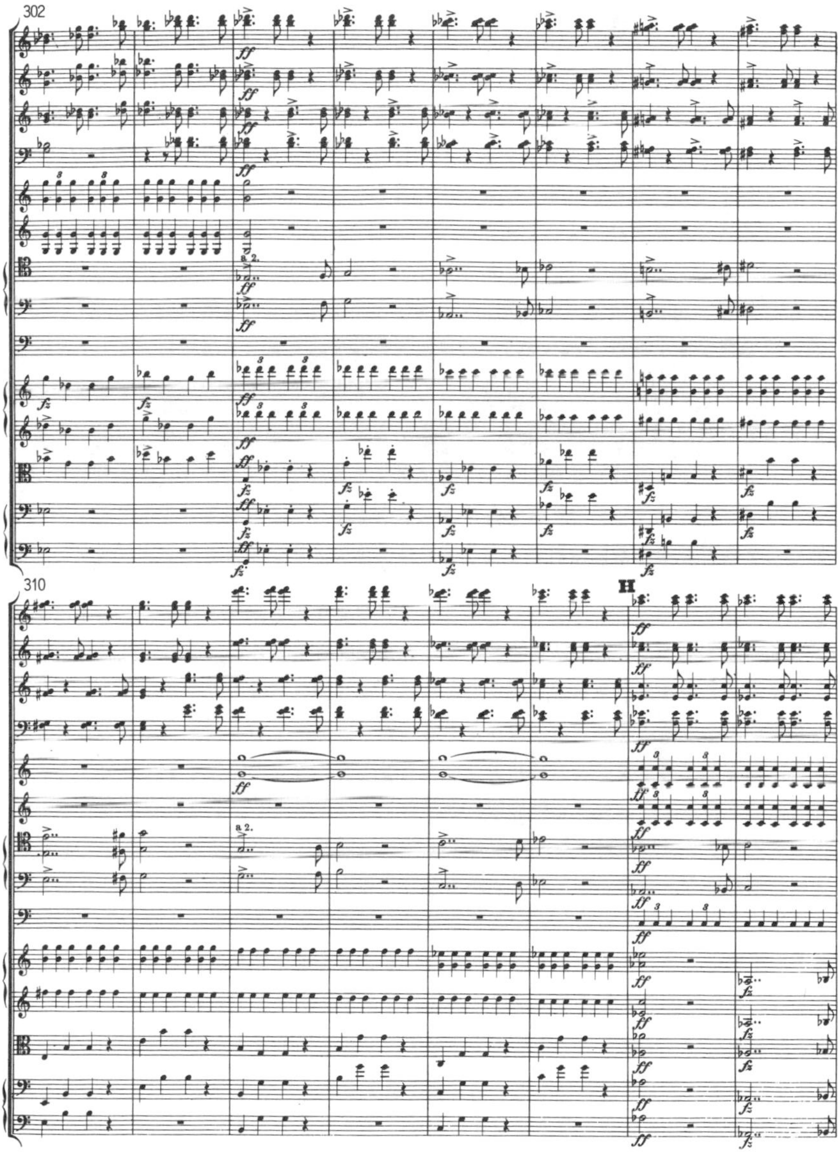
302
310
H
a 2.
ff
fz

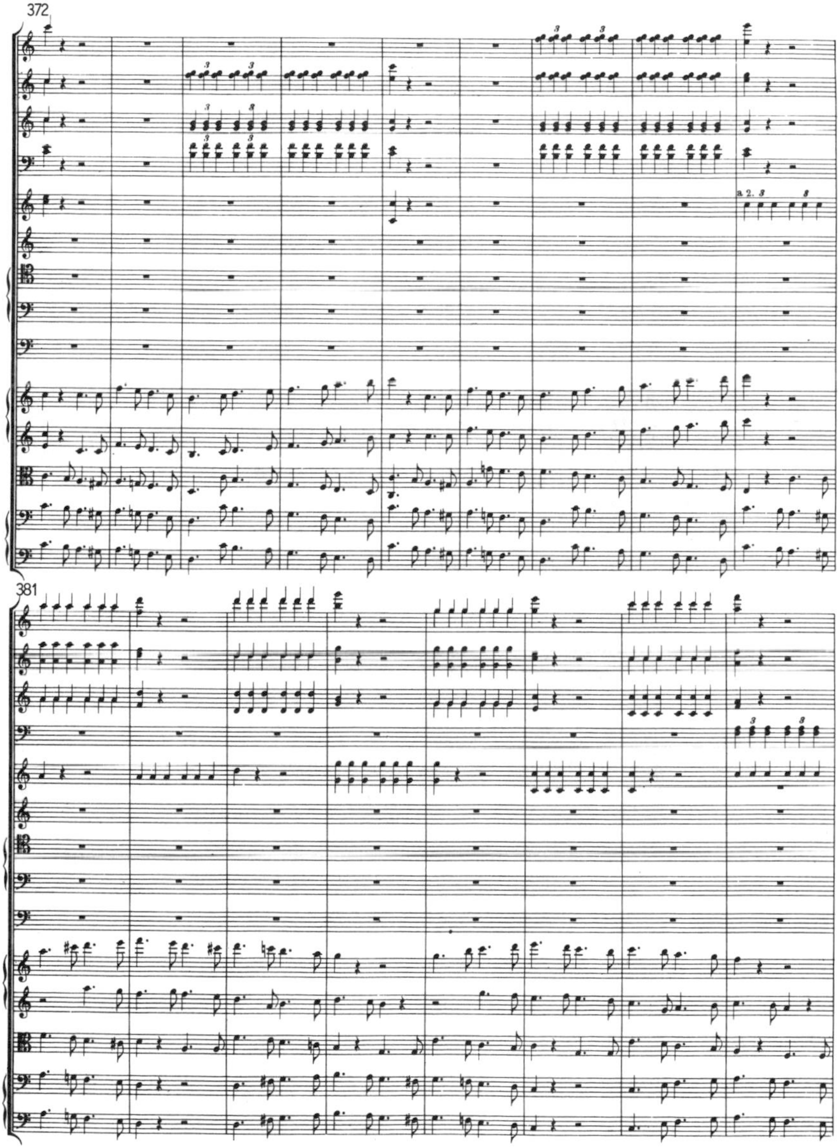
372
381
a 2.

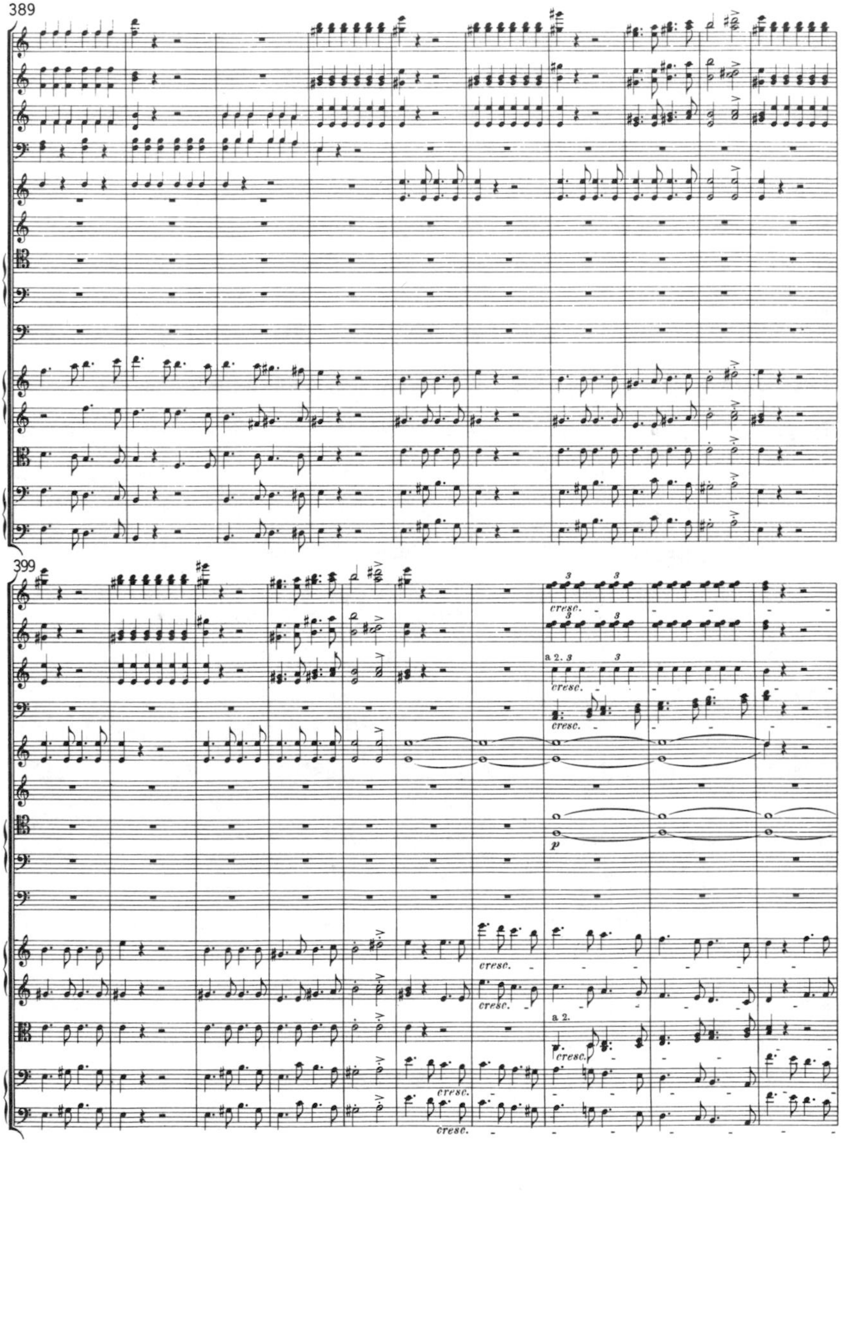
389
399
cresc.
a 2.
p
3

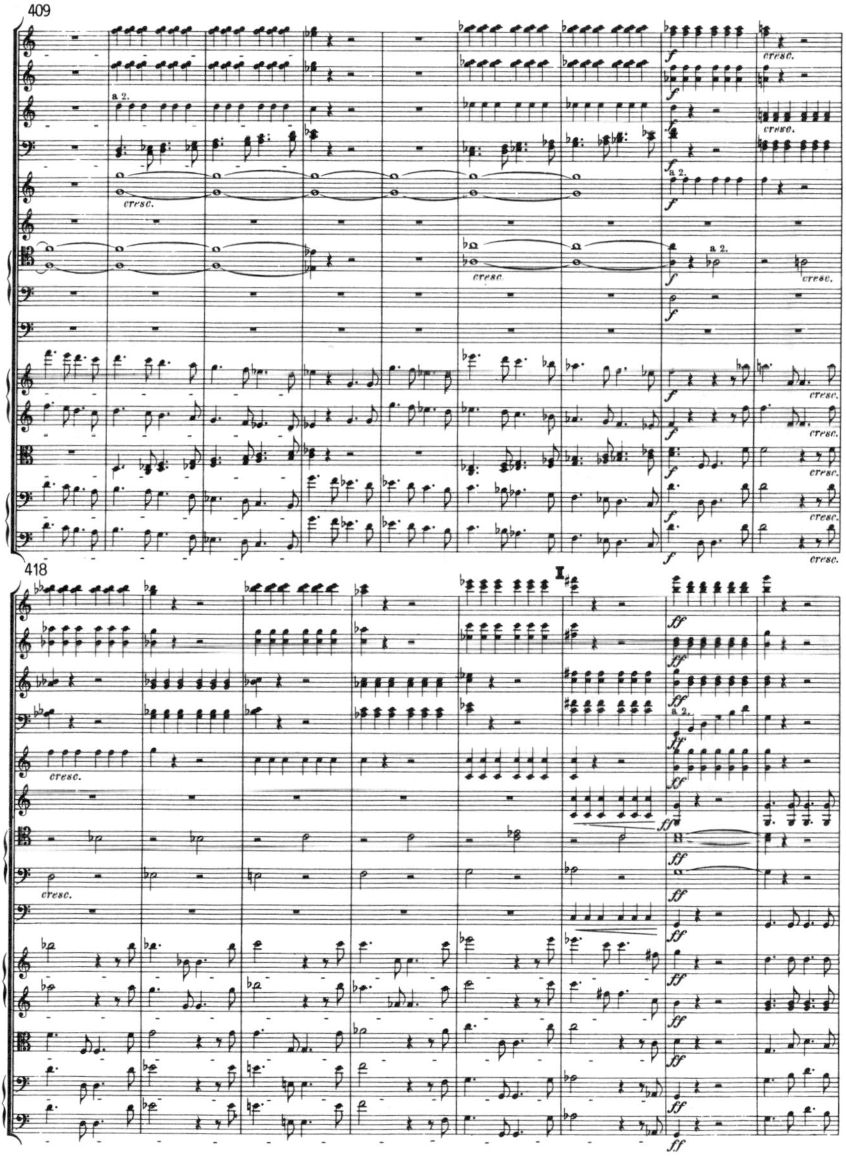
409
a 2.
cresc.
cresc.
f
cresc.
cresc.
a 2.
418
cresc.
cresc.
ff
a 2.

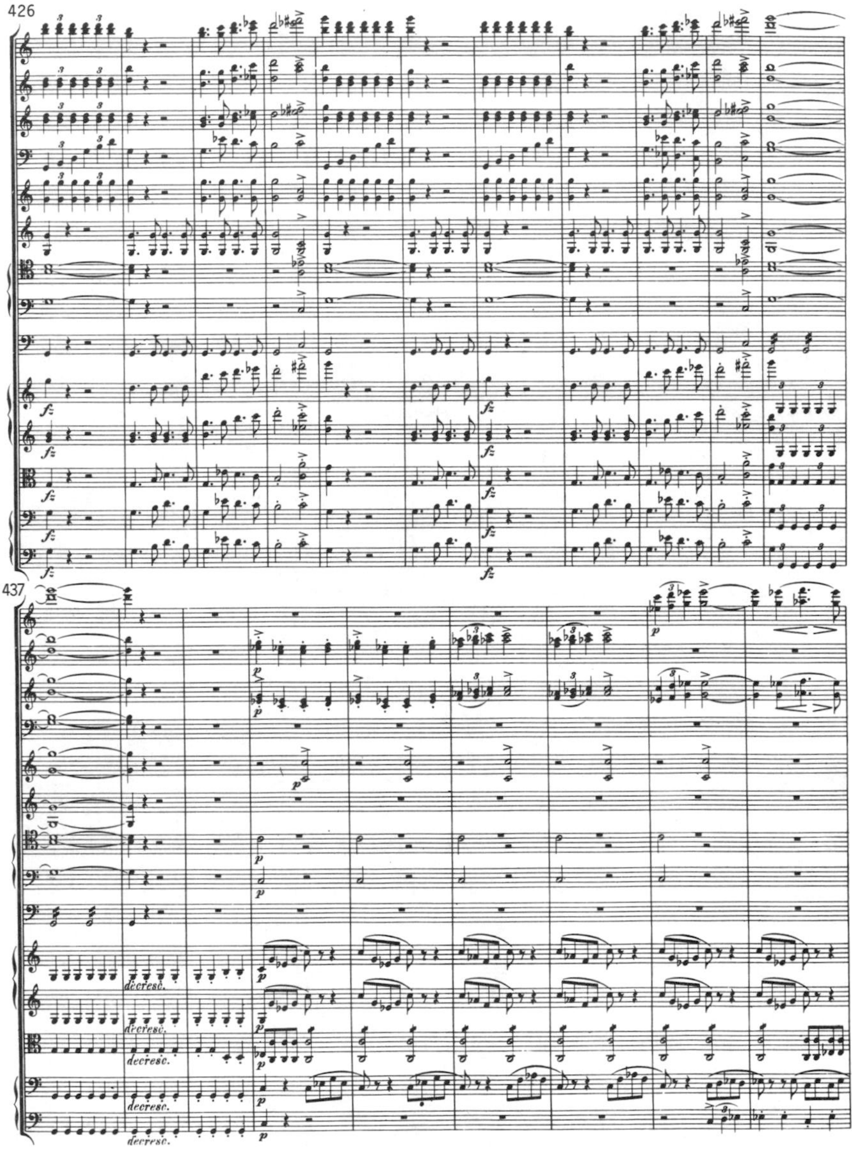
426
437
fz
p
decresc.

Più moto.

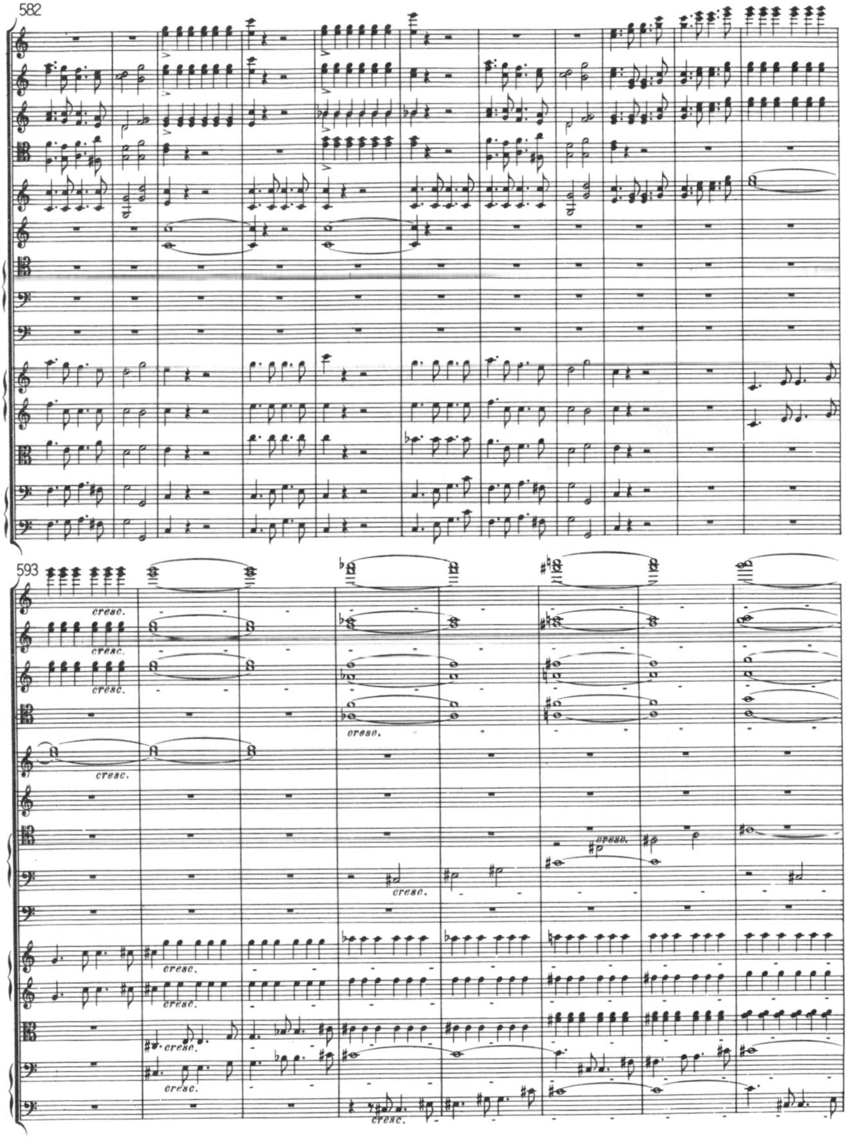
582
593
cresc.

Flauti.

Oboi.

Clarinetti in A.

Fagotti.

Corni in C.

Trombe in A.

Tromboni. { Alto. Tenore. Basso.

Timpani in A.E.

Violino I.

Violino II.

Viola.

Violoncello.

Basso.

Andante con moto.

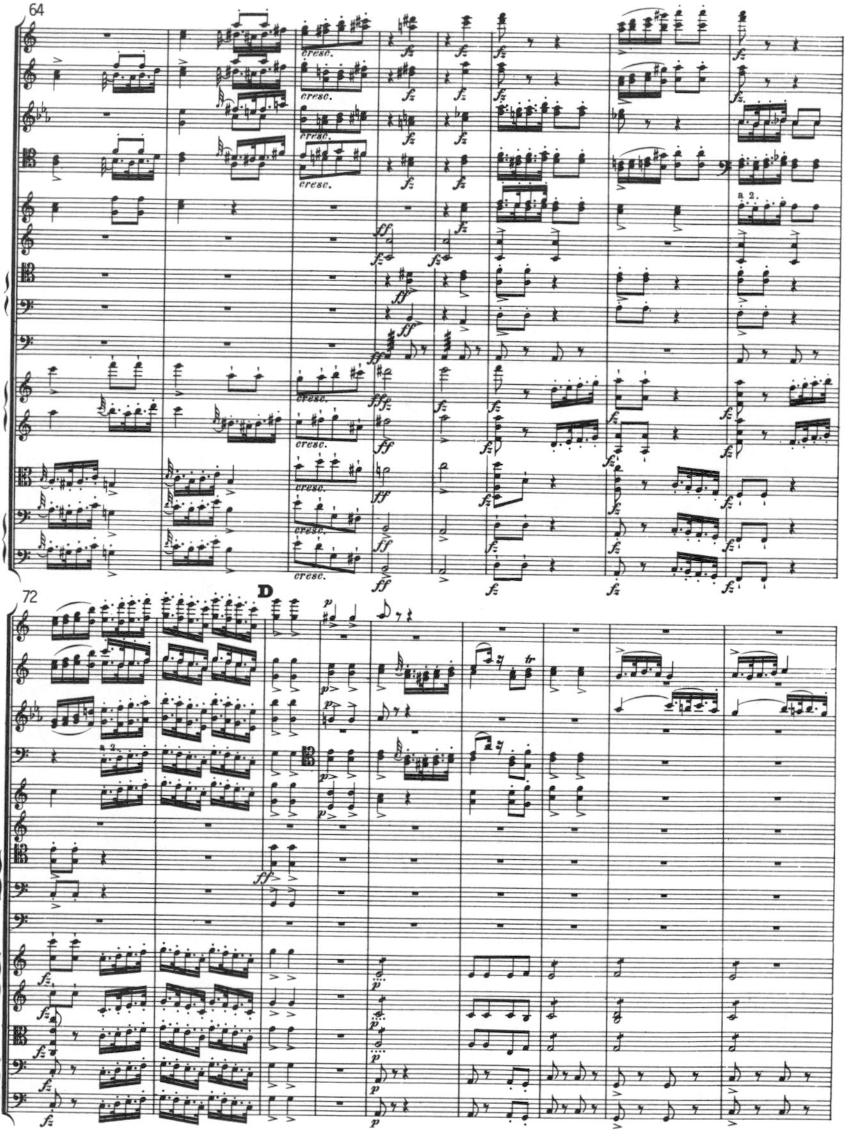
64
cresc.
fz
ff
a 2.
72
D
p
tr

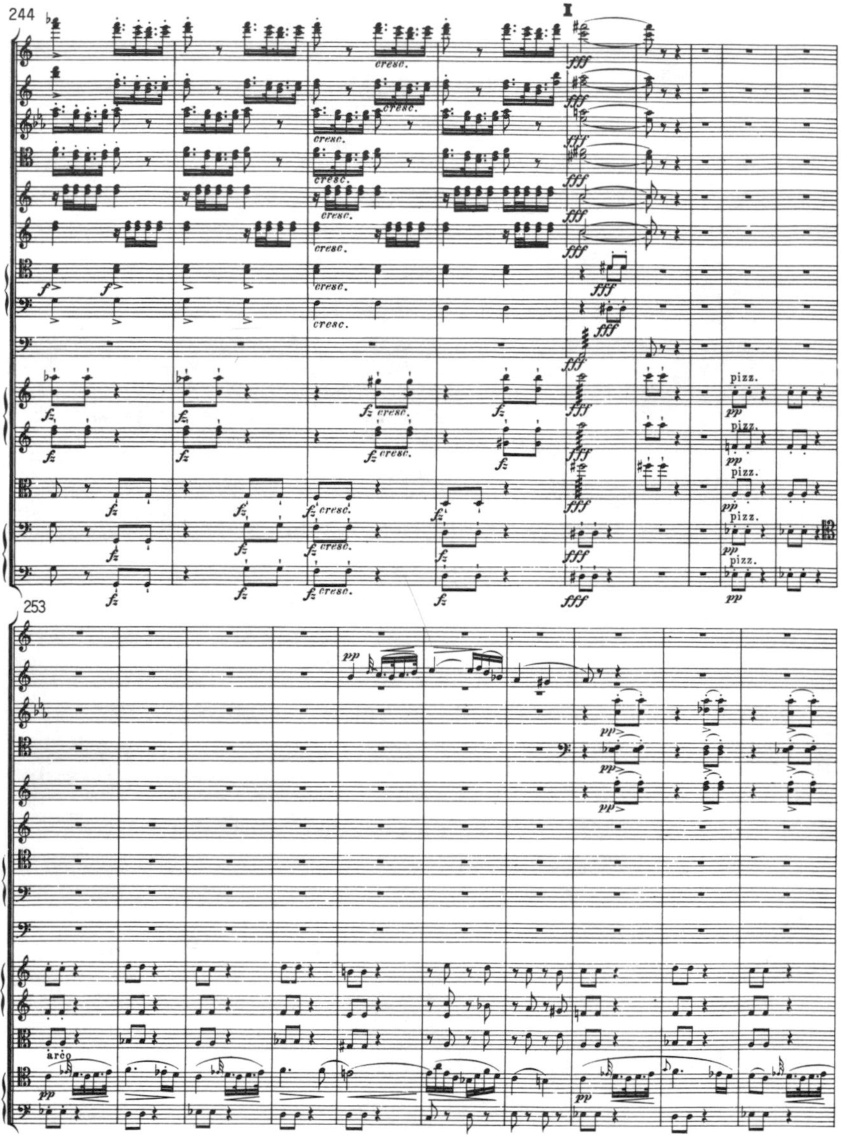
244
I
cresc.
fff
fz
pizz.
pp
253
arco

Scherzo.
Allegro vivace.

Flauti.

Oboi.

Clarinetti in C.

Fagotti.

Corni in C.

Trombe in C,

Alto.
Tenore.
Tromboni.
Basso.

Timpani in C. G.

Violino I.

Violino II.

Viola.

Violoncello.

Basso.

93

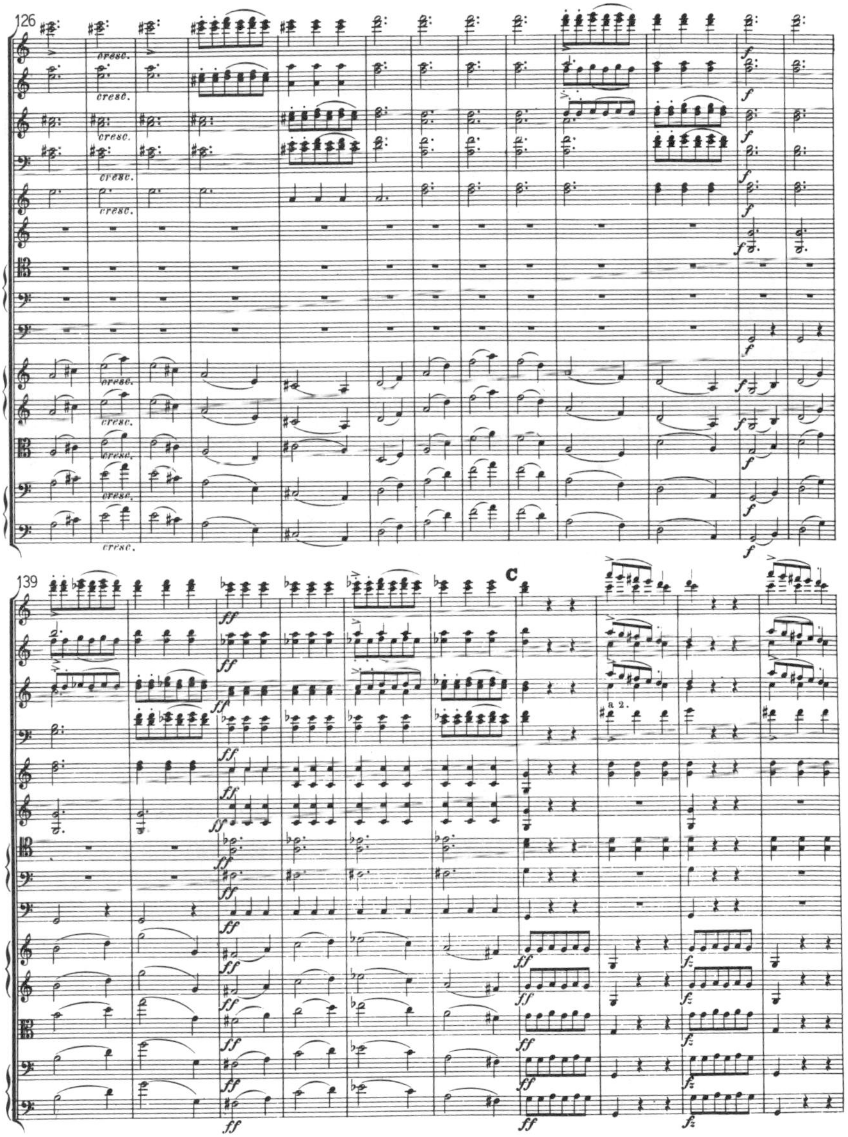
126
cresc.
f
139
ff
C
a 2.
fz

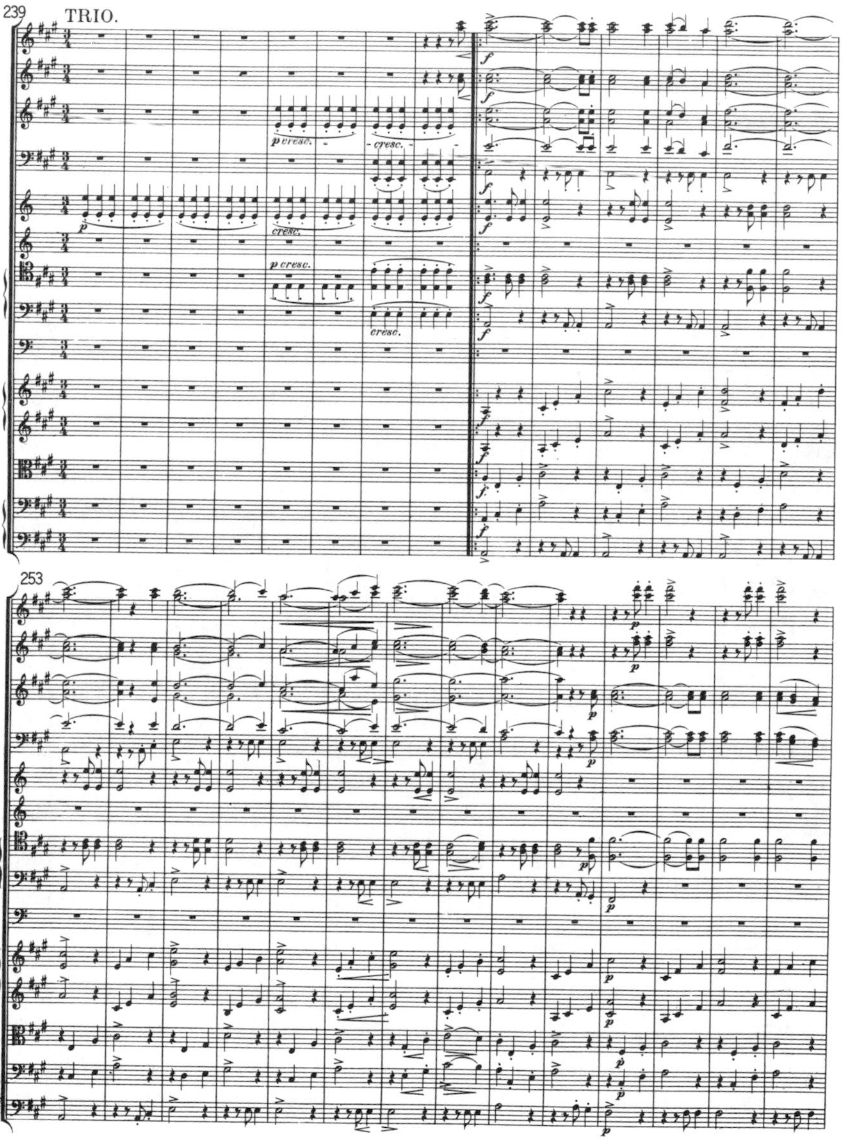
239
TRIO.
p cresc.
cresc.
253

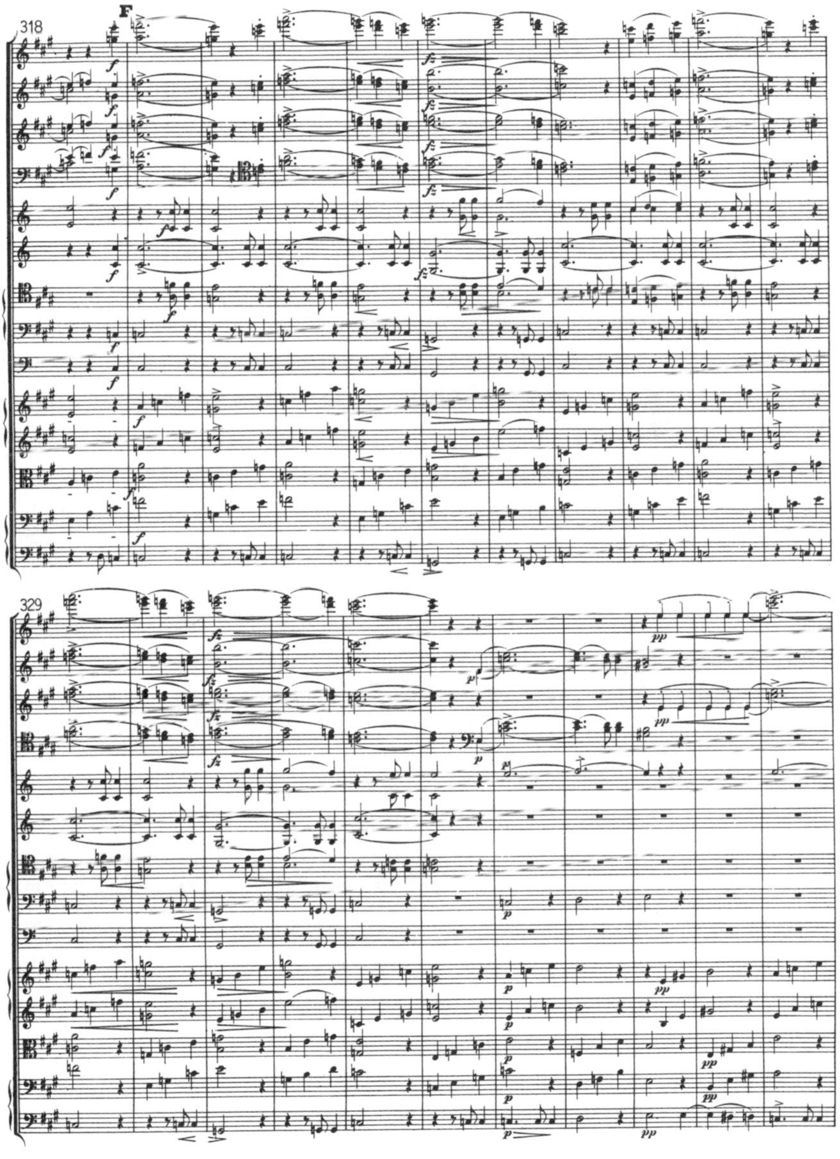
318
F
329

Scherzo D. C.

Allegro vivace.

Flauti.

Oboi.

Clarinetti in C.

Fagotti.

Corni in C.

Trombe in C.

Tromboni. Alto. Tenore. Basso.

Timpani in C.G.

Violino I.

Violino II.

Viola.

Violoncello.

Basso.

110

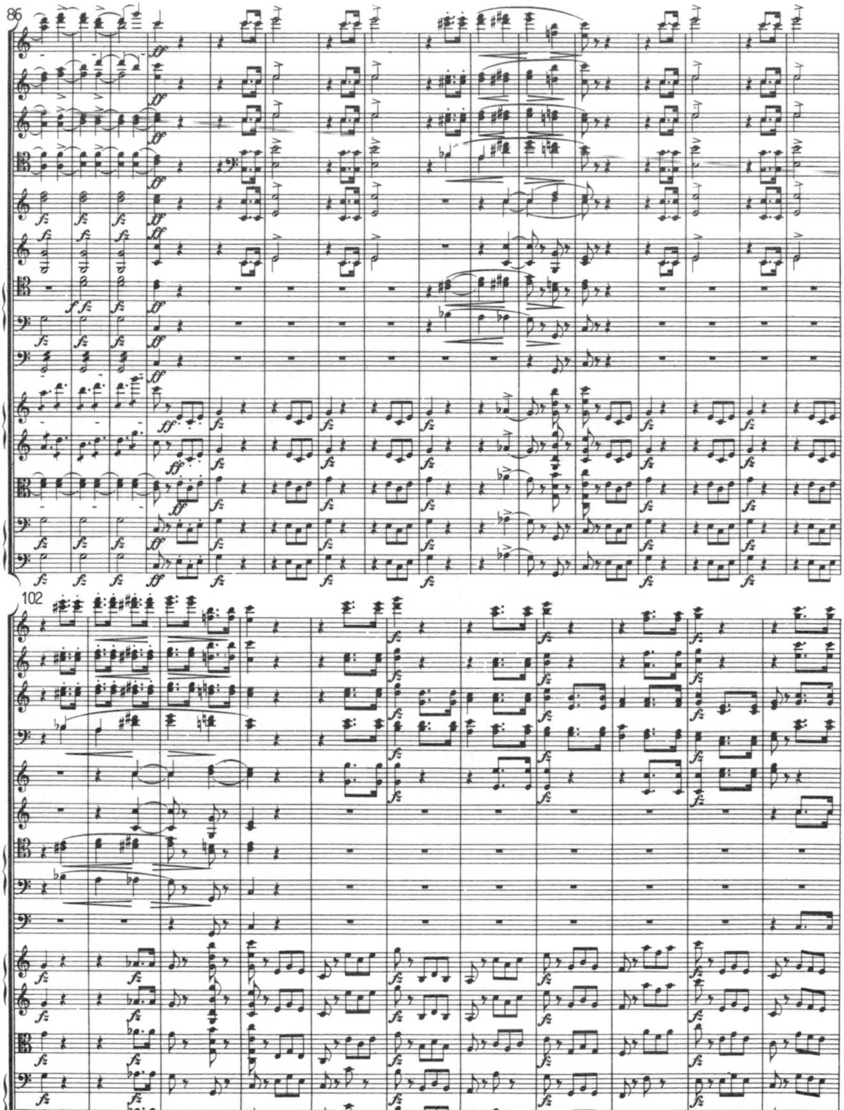
86
102

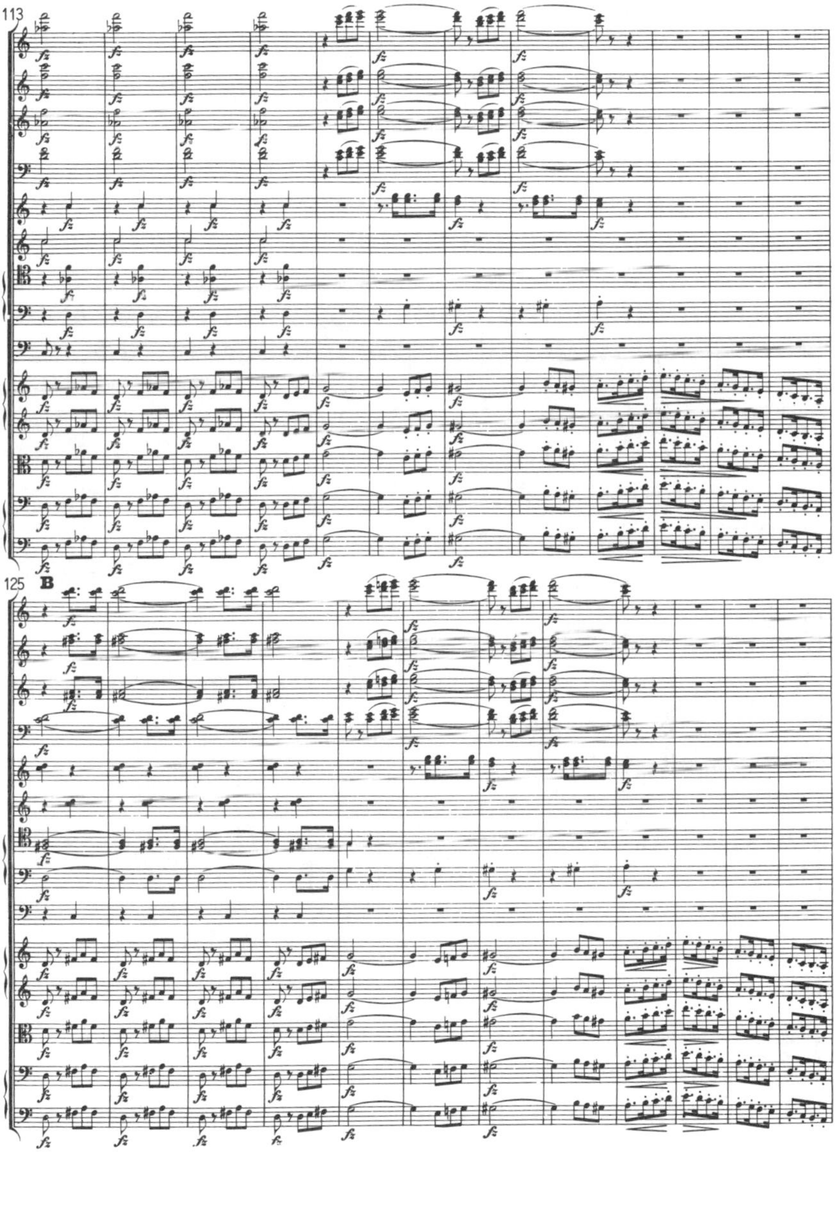
113
125
B

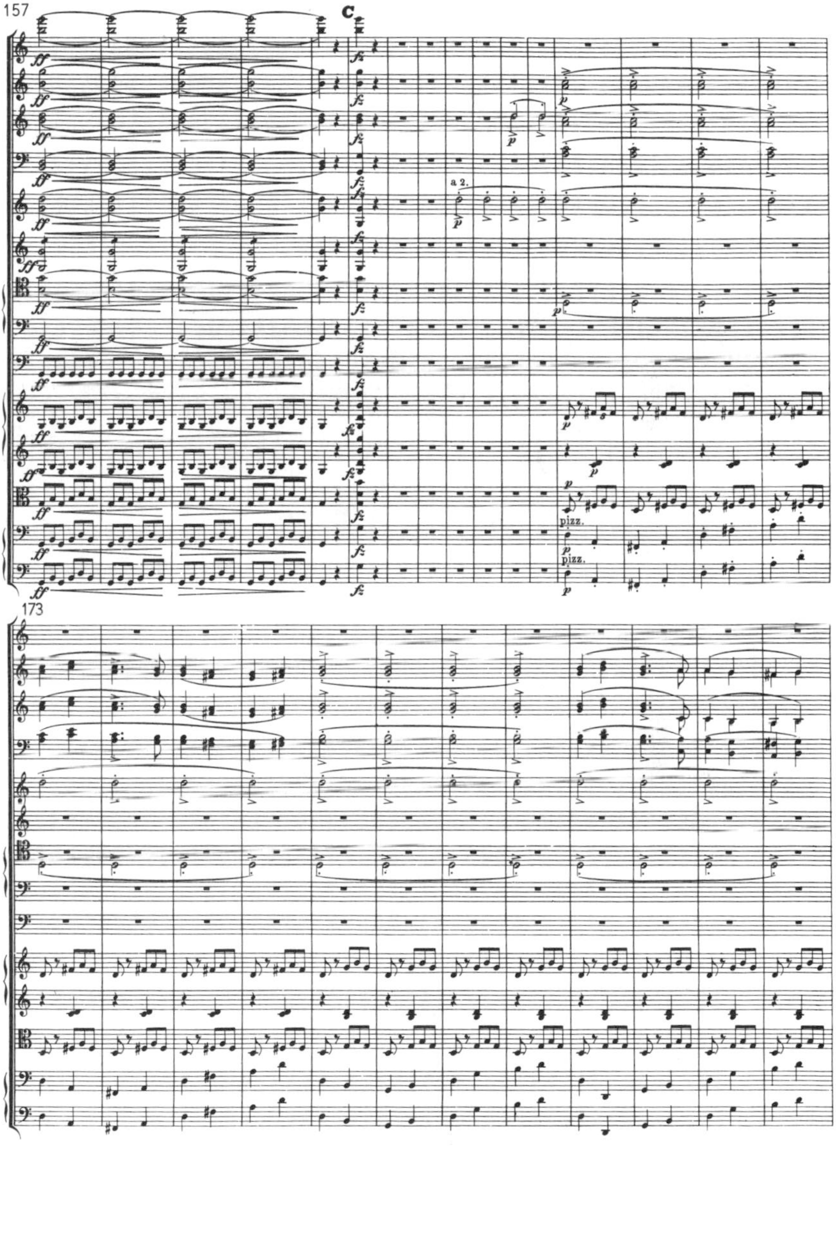
157
C
a 2.
pizz.
pizz.
173

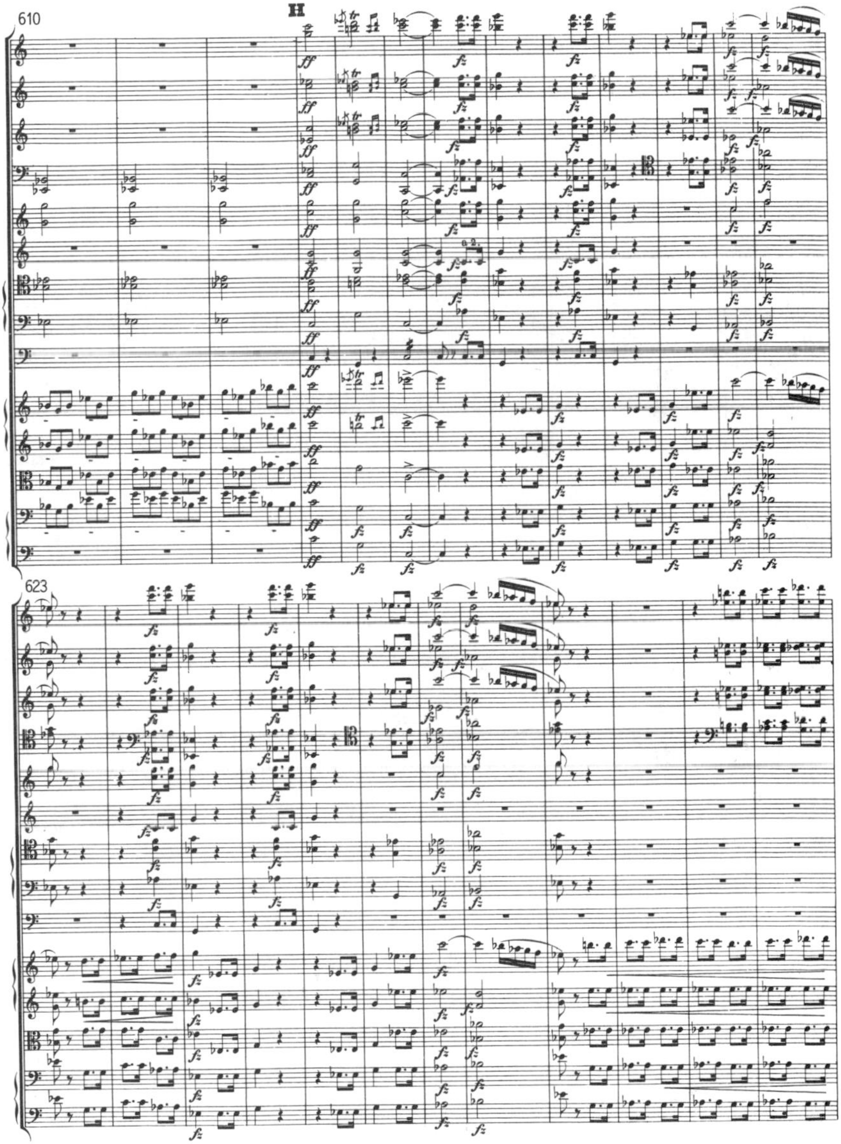
610
H
623

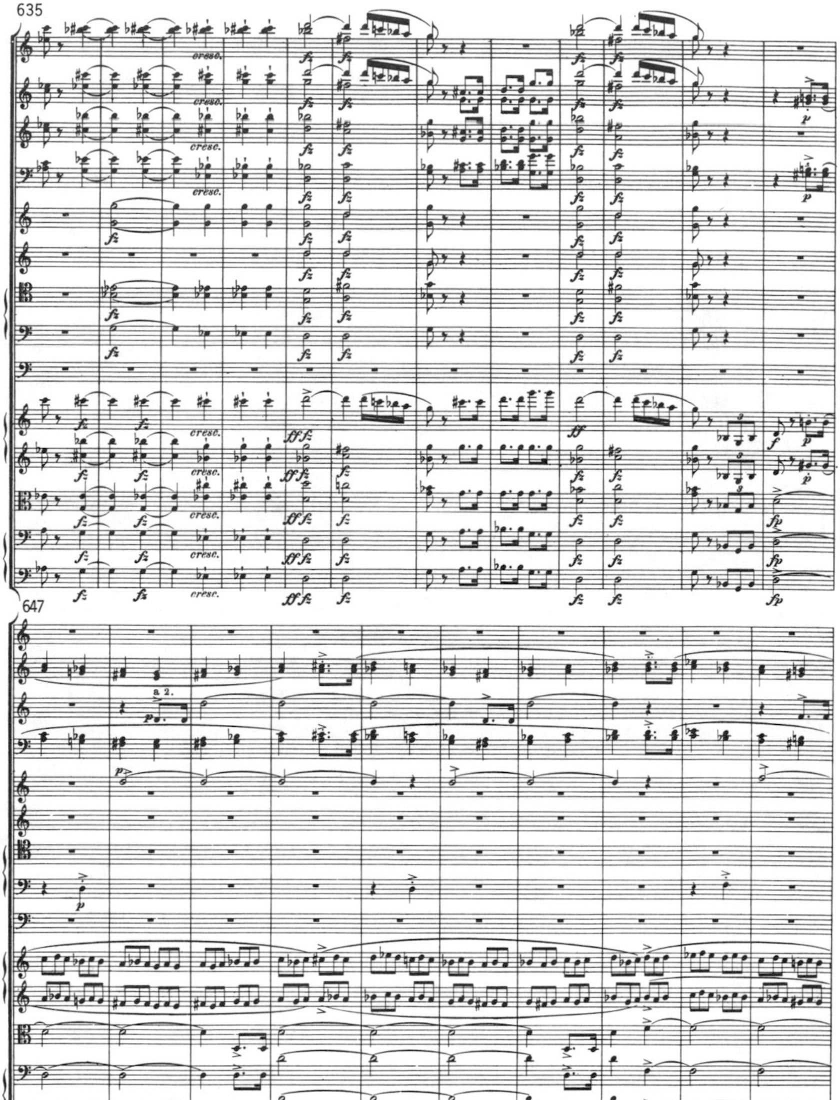
635
cresc.
647
a 2.

657
p cresc.
cresc.
cresc.
cresc.
cresc.
cresc.
cresc.
cresc.
cresc.
cresc.
668
cresc.
cresc.
cresc.
cresc.
cresc.
cresc.
cresc.
f
fz
f
f
f
cresc.
cresc.
cresc.

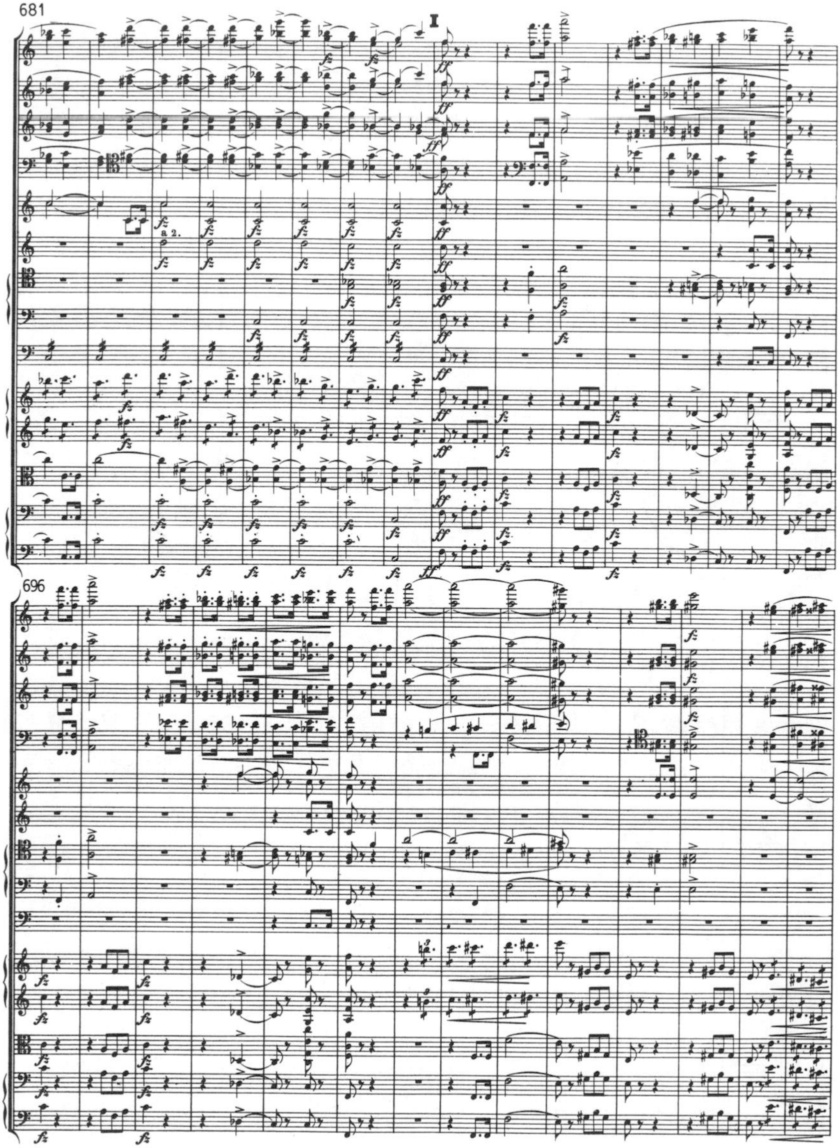
681
I
a 2.
696

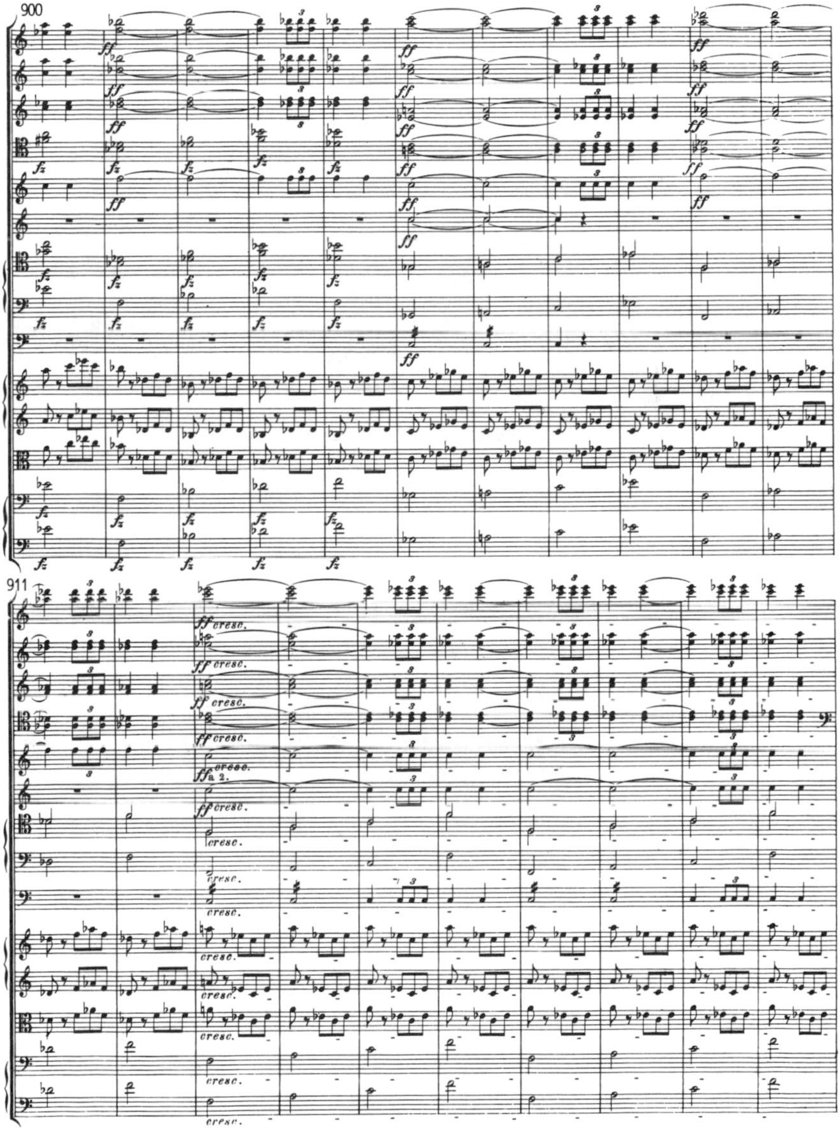
900
911
ff cresc.
a 2.
cresc.

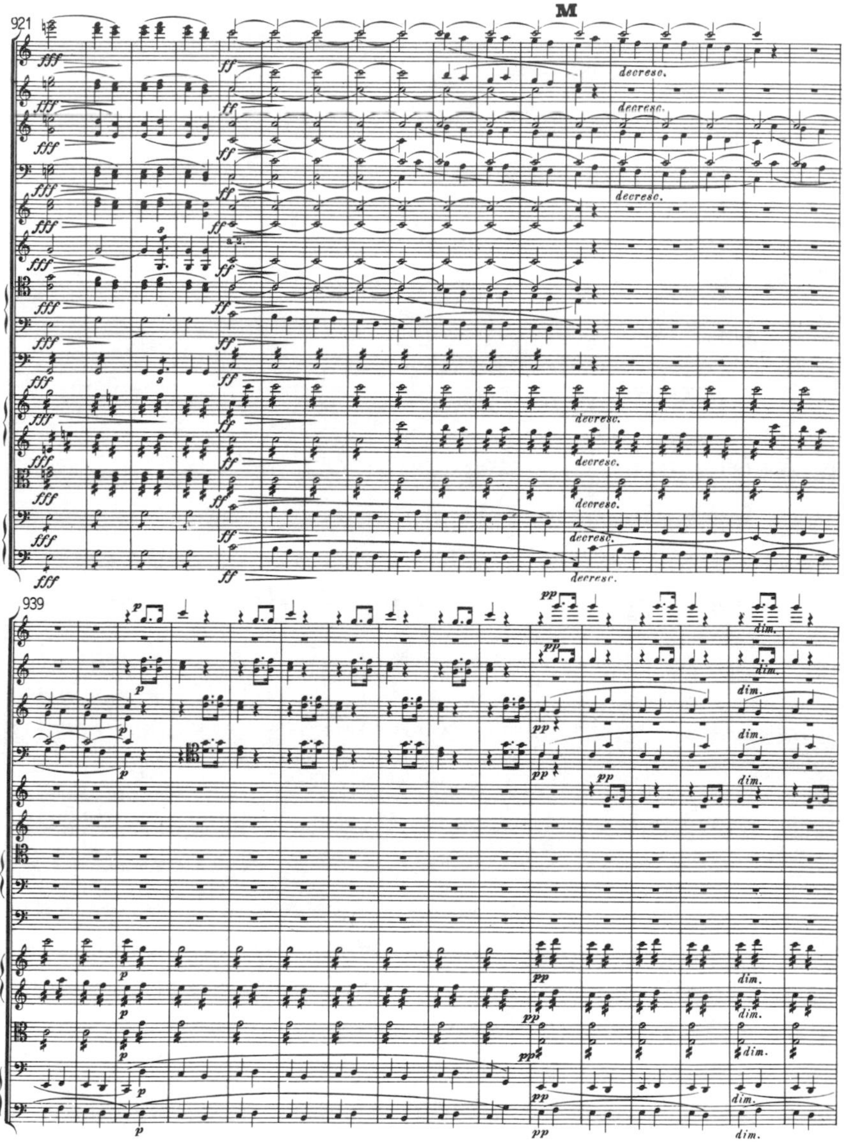
921
M
fff
ff
a 2.
decresc.
939
p
pp
dim.

END OF EDITION